A special gift for

_____

With love from

_____

Date

_____

This gift edition is comprised of excerpts from
The Power of a Positive Wife

Also by Karol Ladd
The Power of a Positive Woman (complete edition)
The Power of a Positive Woman (gift edition)
The Power of a Positive Mom (complete edition)
The Power of a Positive Mom (gift edition)
The Power of a Positive Friend (complete edition)
The Power of a Positive Friend (gift edition)
The Power of a Positive Wife (complete edition)

FROM THE BEST-SELLING *Power of a Positive* SERIES

Karol Ladd

GIFT EDITION

THe
Power
OF A
Positive
Wife

HOWARD
PUBLISHING CO.

Our purpose at Howard Publishing is to:

• *Increase faith* in the hearts of growing Christians

• *Inspire holiness* in the lives of believers

• *Instill hope* in the hearts of struggling people everywhere

Because He's coming again!

The Power of a Positive Wife, Gift Edition © 2004 by Karol Ladd
All rights reserved. Printed in the United States of America

Published by Howard Publishing Co., Inc.
3117 North 7th Street, West Monroe, Louisiana 71291-2227
www.howardpublishing.com

04 05 06 07 08 09 10 11 12 13   10 9 8 7 6 5 4 3 2

Cover and interior design by LinDee Loveland and Stephanie D. Walker

ISBN: 1-58229-363-5

The most important
ingredient
in the recipe for a great wife is

God-centeredness

(not husband-centeredness).
First and foremost,
a great wife is
a godly woman.

1

A God-centered wife enjoys
her relationship with her husband,
understanding that both husband
and wife are God-given
complements to one another.
She finds her
joy, peace, and
inner strength
from the only true source: God.

Our value doesn't come
from how well we perform.
It's based on
our faith–
on our recognition that the gifts and
talents we have are from God
and that without God
we are nothing.

"Becoming one" doesn't mean
losing who we are as individuals.
It means *using* who we are as

individuals

to strengthen the marriage.

Wives were created by God
for a significant plan and purpose.
Creation wasn't complete until the
wife was brought on the scene.
That means you and I have a

powerful and important

place in this world!

Divide a piece of paper in half.

List

some of your
strengths and weaknesses
on one half. On the other, list the
strengths and weaknesses your
husband has that complement or
help equalize yours.
Notice how God has made you a
good fit for one another.

6

Marvelous Creator,
thank You
for my husband. Thank You for the
strengths and weaknesses we both
bring into our marriage.

Help us to complement,
bless, and serve each other.
Most importantly, keep my heart and
mind focused on You.

As positive wives, we must

choose

to live a godly life;
the good news is
that we don't have to live it
by our own power.
We have God's glorious power
working in and through us.

Giving control

of our lives to God doesn't mean we
let go of our responsibilities.
It simply means
we leave the worry and
the results to God.

9

We may see flaws and weaknesses
in our husbands and think it's our
job to take control
and change their ways.

But that's not our job;
it's God's.

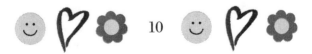

Challenges

and struggles

take on a different air when we
see them in light of eternity.
The Sculptor's sharp chisel may be
just the thing that fashions us into a

beautiful work of art.

11

Devote one day
this week to
dwelling
in God's presence
all day long, even as you go about
your normal routine. You may want
to make it a day of fasting (from food
or sweets or soft drinks) as a way of
reminding yourself to walk
continuously in His presence.

 12

Heavenly Father,

may Your power work through my weaknesses and

make a positive impact on my marriage,

my home, and my community.

13

Marriage Myths

1. There is one "true love" out there for me. I must find him, marry him, and live happily ever after.

2. In order to love others, I must first love myself.

3. I can fall out of love with my spouse.

True-Love
Principles

1. True love is not simply discovered; it is created, and it takes work.

2. Loving my spouse is not based on my own self-love but on understanding my value from God's perspective.

3. Marital love is a commitment encompassing affection, friendship, pleasure, and selfless love.

 15

True love
doesn't mean having
a relationship of ease;
it means making the

continual choice

to love and forgive.

As positive wives,
let's not build our houses
on myths but on the
rock-solid truth
of God's love.

 17

Schedule

an evening or Saturday-
morning walk
with your husband.
Talk together about how our culture
defines love. Identify some
misconceptions, then discuss how
you would define love and
how you can better show
that love to each other.

Father of Mercy,

pour Your beautiful and abundant love through me. Give me the power to love my husband with patience and kindness.

Let me be a reflection of Your love in my home.

Forgiveness

is an act of the will and
an attitude of the heart.
It's a choice we make not to hold
resentment toward the offender. It is
a release of our right to be angry.

When you
choose
to let go of bitterness
or resentment
toward your husband—
even if you think you have a right to
feel that way—your spouse gets a
fresh beginning.
He is free to make new choices,
better ones.

Responsibility

is demanded on the part of both the

forgiver and the forgiven.

Yes, we must forgive our husbands.
But if we see them mired in habitual
or continual sin, we must love them
enough to help them get out of it.

  22

Ask God

to reveal any areas of
unforgiveness in your heart.
Then *recognize* the unforgiveness,
realize you have no right to hold on to
it, *release* bitterness and anger, *resume*
your relationship with a clean slate,
and help *restore* your spouse if he is
in destructive behavior patterns.

Father, thank You for Your love
and forgiveness.

Help me

to pour this forgiveness out
to everyone around me,
especially to my husband.
Help me to release any resentment
I have toward my spouse
and to love him by forgiving him
as I have been forgiven.

24

Commitment
is a form of glue
that holds a marriage together.

   25

People aren't easy
to live with.
As Christians we're called to

persevere

through the tough times,
whether we feel "happy" or not.
Scripture warns us that life is not
going to be great all the time.

26

What would happen if we looked at
our spouses' differences
and our marital difficulties and
asked ourselves,

what does God want me
to learn
from this relationship?
How does He want me to grow in
this situation in order to make me
more like Christ?

27

As positive wives

we must choose to love *through* the
difficulties and *past* the differences.

We must make a conscious choice

to overlook our husbands' faults and
focus on their potential.

Write a love note

to your husband.
Tell him how glad you are to be
married to him and list some of the
qualities he possesses that make you
thankful. Close by telling him
you are committed to him
for the rest of your life.

Eternal, heavenly Father,
thank You
for never giving up
on me. Help me to persevere
in my love for my husband.
Keep us faithful to our marriage
vows until death do us part.

There is wisdom in choosing not to take every issue to battle.

Some things are worth fighting for; **some things are not.**

The Rules of
Engagement

1. Listen more than you talk. (James 1:19)

2. Remain calm; keep your voice down. (Proverbs 15:1)

3. Keep current; leave old issues behind. (Philippians 3:13)

4. Avoid condescending phrases or character attacks. (Ephesians 4:29–32)

The best arguments
have two results:
a diminishing of the initial conflict
and an understanding of one
another's perspective.
That's not win-lose;

that's win-win!

When an issue comes
between you and your husband,
try to see the matter with

spiritual eyes.

Your husband is not the enemy; Satan is.
Join with your husband and

work together to find
a resolution.

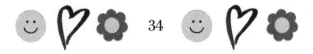

On a piece of paper,
write out
the Rules of Engagement
listed on page 32. Look up the
scriptures and jot down some notes
on the key points. Frame and
memorize these important tips for
handling disagreements with
dignity and grace.

Father, thank You for my
wonderful
husband.

Help us to work through our
conflicts in a positive way. Unify us
so that we work together against the
conflict and not against each other.
Bring us continually back together
again in love and forgiveness.

We can
value and respect
our husbands
because God made them.
They are designed and fashioned
by our loving, heavenly Father.

As positive wives,

we shouldn't wait

for our husbands to show us love
before we act;

we must move forward
and show respect anyway.

Many times a loving reaction
will follow.

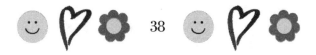

38

Respect

is a gift

wrapped in the beautiful paper of kind words and tied with the enormous ribbon of a loving spirit. It is a pouring out of ourselves. It's going beyond what we want and offering our husbands what they need. It is not an easy gift to give.

39

Respect is a powerful tool.
When a wife respects her husband,
he moves forward, knowing that the
person who is closest to him sees his
potential and backs him up.

It's a powerful thing

to have someone support
you and believe in you.

Reflect

on your relationship
with your husband.
Ask God to reveal any ways in which
you show your husband disrespect
and to help you esteem your
husband in those areas. Look for
opportunities to show your husband
that you respect him.

41

Lord, thank You for my husband.
Help me to give him
the gift of
respect.

Use that respect to build him up and
encourage him to pursue Your
calling in his life. Work in his life
and mine, allowing us to become all
You've created us to be.

A positive attitude
is not a feeling
but an underlying outlook
we have toward people
and toward life. It represents
a hope and faith that is rooted
within our hearts.

We have the
power to color
the situations in our lives
by our attitudes. Will we choose
to see the world in

hopeful hues,

or will we choose to paint our
challenges in gloomy gray?

We all have things we wish were different in our lives, in our marriages, and with our spouses. But the if-only disease will eat us up inside and foster an angry disrespect for our husbands.

We must

choose daily

not to give in to it.

A smile

is a wonderful way to
uplift people.

It's also a wonderful way to lift our
own attitudes. Try giving the gift
of a smile to your husband and the
other people around you
for an entire day, and see how good
it makes you feel!

46

Choose one day
this week to ban worry,
grumbling, and whining
from your heart, mind, and mouth.
Replace those bad habits
with thankfulness, joy, prayer, and
hope. Give your husband
the gift of your smile.

47

Wonderful Lord, my rock and

my refuge,

turn my heart toward You

when I am worried or discouraged.
Help me to be content in the
circumstances I cannot change,
relying always on Christ's strength.
May my attitude reflect my faith in
Your redemptive power.

When our husbands are wrong,
we can have a positive,

powerful impact

by showing them

respect as persons,

even as we make clear
that we don't endorse
what they're doing.

Sometimes we try to cover for our husbands when they're caught in a rut—but all that does is help them stay in the rut! Instead, we must

carefully help

them out of the pit
they're in and encourage
them to pursue a more positive,
healthy lifestyle.

When a wife makes an effort to point
out something her

husband is doing

right,

rather than everything
he's doing wrong,

she spurs him on to

become a better man

and a better husband.

The refining that comes from being married to an imperfect person has lasting value.

It's only in shifting our focus from our husbands' faults to our

Father's work

that we truly become positive wives.

52

Write a prayer

asking God to help you work through the difficult issues in your marriage. Pour your heart out concerning your struggles, especially regarding your husband's wrong behavior.* Read Psalm 40 and take in these healing words.

If your husband's problems place you or your family in a dangerous situation, please seek counseling and help immediately.

Gracious, merciful Father,
thank You for looking past
the sin in my life to see

my potential.

Help me to see past my husband's
problems and recognize his
potential. Help me to honor him
with my words and actions.

54

What we say

can have a significant,
lasting impact on others—

especially our spouses. If we choose
to speak encouraging words, we can
build better marriage relationships,
lift up our husbands, and help them
to reach greater heights.

55

When we first begin giving out daily doses of encouragement, we may need to remind ourselves to dole them out each day. But once

encouragement

becomes a habit, positive, life-giving words will flow more naturally.

If we will start
noticing and encouraging
our husbands'

positive qualities,

many of the negatives will begin
to diminish and take care of
themselves.

Why should we get stuck giving
the same encouragement over and over
when we have so many areas
to choose from each day?
If we will use a little variety,

our daily dose of
encouragement can always be
**fresh, new,
and real.**

 58

Place a note

somewhere you (and only you)
will see it to
remind yourself

to speak at least one word of
encouragement to your husband
each day. Make a deliberate effort
to build your marriage by
encouraging your husband in
sincere and creative ways.

59

Father, You are the

Great Encourager.

Keep me from having
a critical spirit and
help me to focus on my
husband's strengths.
Help me to be a blessing to him,
building him up and helping him
to be the best he can be.

One of the main ways we
can deepen our

relationships

with our spouses is to discover
creative ways to

enjoy each other's
company.

Don't close the door on new
activities. You may be surprised.
Try it, you may like it;
and if you don't, move on.
The important thing is to be

continually open

to ways you can share
companionship
with your husband.

Our number one job as creative
companions is to

prayerfully seek

God's imaginative wisdom
for building our marriages.
If we ask, He will help us
identify fresh and new ways to
deepen our harmony and
companionship with our spouses.

Sharing

on a spiritual level

will bond you and your husband
in a deep way. Pray together for your
family, for your future plans
and upcoming activities,
and for your relationship.

  64

Plot several potential

date nights

on the calendar.

Talk to your husband and have him choose the one that works best for him. On your date remember to gaze at each other, touch, smile, and discuss plans for just the two of you.

65

Lord, help me

to enjoy my relationship with my
husband. Show me new
and creative ways to

develop our companionship
more fully.

Deepen the love and
delight we have in each other.

When we take care of ourselves and
make the effort to look
our best, *we*
feel better.

We're more confident and assured.
The key is to keep a balanced
perspective.

The greatest beauty

radiates from within.
A godly, gracious, loving, honest,
and positive woman offers
an unsurpassed gift of loveliness
to her spouse.

68

The problem with comparing ourselves with others is that there will always be someone more attractive and someone less attractive. Our goal is not to look more beautiful than the next girl but to

look our best by taking care of ourselves.

Stand confidently

in the knowledge that God
has made you in
His image
and fashioned you for a purpose.
All the fluff you do on the outside
simply enhances the beauty already
inherent in you because
you are His creation.

70

Look in the mirror and evaluate your "wrapping." Are there any changes you want to make? Now look in the mirror of God's Word by reading Galatians 5:22–23. Do you reflect the beauty of a godly spirit in your attitude and actions?

Enhance your beauty by spending time with God each day.

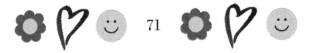

71

Glorious Creator, You have fashioned
me just the way You want me. You
have a plan and a purpose for my life.

Help me to be

beautiful inside

and out by producing in me the
beautiful qualities of love, joy,
peace, patience, kindness, goodness,
faithfulness, gentleness,
and self-control.

Lovemaking

enriches and deepens
the commitment and communion
between a man and a woman
who've given themselves to
one another in marriage.

Sexual intimacy is a

giving

of ourselves to our spouses.
It's not a reward to be given or
withheld in order to control,
manipulate, or show our husbands
we're hurt about something.

  74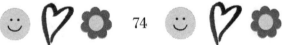

Be a tiger!

Enjoy the blessings,
pleasures, and benefits

of a fulfilling marriage and
an intimate sex life as you and your
husband grow in your love
for one another.

75

The best sex takes place between
two people who have

committed

their lives to one another, who love
each other so much that they

only seek each other's
pleasure.

76

Plan a
romantic night
at home with your
husband.
(Make arrangements for the kids to
be at Grandma's or a friend's house.)
Begin the day by hinting to him
about the pleasure that is to come.
Create your own romantic adventure.

Lord, thank You for my husband and
for the beautiful gift of sex that
You have given us in marriage.
Help us to

faithfully love

and enjoy each other all
the days of our lives.
Show us how to be each other's
mate, helper, lover, and friend.

 78

As positive wives,
we want to make sure that

money is a tool

we use wisely to build a
solid foundation
and a secure future for our families.
We don't want unwise financial
decisions to wreck the peace
in our marriages and
undercut our future plans.

Don't get caught in the trap of always wanting more. Ask God to

help you develop a

heart

of contentment.

Being content doesn't mean we never fulfill our wants; it means we make our purchasing decisions based on wisdom and sound financial practices, not on emotion.

Through Christ's strength,
when we are tempted to want
the here-and-now,
we can keep our eyes

focused

on things of eternal value.

81

Whatever financial mistakes
we may have made in the past,
let's determine to

start today

to be a blessing to our
husbands and families

by being responsible with the
resources God has given us.

Go over financial matters
with your husband.

Decide together

what spending, saving, and
budgeting plans are best for your
family. Identify ways each of you
can adjust or change to meet the
common goal of financial
responsibility.

God, You are the Great Provider.
Thank You that I can look to You for
help and direction in my finances.
Help me to be responsible in my
spending and saving. Most importantly,

help me to be

content

no matter what my

circumstances are.

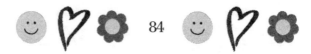

There is no right or wrong way to
figure out who does what.
The important thing is for you and
your husband to have a

mutual understanding
of one another's

roles

as you work through the
responsibilities of your
household together.

 85

Look for solutions
to make your life together
less stressful.
If possible, pay someone else
to do a chore so your time and energy
can go into activities
you need to do yourself.

86

When dividing
domestic tasks,
take into account the unique gifts,
abilities, and talents
each of you possesses.

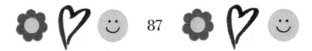

As positive wives, we can fulfill our
many responsibilities in and out
of our homes with continuous joy
because we know that we answer
ultimately to God.
He's our Employer,
and if we're faithful, one
day we'll hear Him say,
"Well done."

List the activities

in which you are
currently involved.
Are there any areas that need to
change? Should you be doing more,
or do you need to slow down?
Talk it over with your husband; he
may have a unique perspective
and some good ideas.

Lord, thank You for the abilities and
talents You've given me.
Help me to use these gifts in my
home and my community.
Make me a blessing to all those
around me, especially my husband.
Help me to maintain a

healthy balance

in my life.

Nothing is more vital to a
positive marriage
than a wife's
commitment to prayer.
How foolish we are when we try
to hold our marriages together
without the presence of God!

As we do the laundry,
clean the house, and run errands,
we can walk and
talk with God.
At work, at school, at soccer games,
we can continue
to commune with Him.

If we're going to
be successful

in our marriages and effective
in all the things God has called us
to do, we need to

ask for His help.

93

Meeting with God each day
is better than any beauty treatment
money can buy.
A wife who meets with God, relishes
His love, and casts her cares on Him
will have a demeanor of

confidence and
brightness

that everyone around her will see.

The key to a holy, happy, and
beautiful life is a lifestyle of prayer
and intimate fellowship with God.

As positive wives,

let's be
praying wives.

That way we'll be sure to shine.

Set aside a time
and choose a place to
meet with God each day.

Then start meeting. This takes
discipline, so be diligent.
In your quiet moments with the
Lord, delight in Him! That's the key
to a peaceful, joyful,
and holy life.

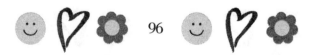

Wonderful Father,

thank You for hearing
my prayers.
I want to walk closely with You
each day. My desire is for You, and
my longing is for intimate fellowship
with You. Keep my heart on things
above, and do not let me stray from
Your principles.

The Bible is more than
a love letter; it's the

instruction
manual

for life, written by
the very Maker of life.

As you read and meditate daily on
God's Word, you will

grow

to know God in a deeper
and more intimate way.
You'll glean wisdom and direction
for life and find comfort and
hope for the journey.

Our charge as positive wives is to

meditate

on God's Word day and night.
That's the key to
our success.

100

Choose a book
of the Bible
to read, study, and
meditate upon.

Read a portion every day. Ask God
to teach you from His Word. Use a
journal to record insights or
questions. Commit a verse from
that passage to memory.

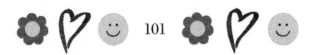

101

Father, help me to be

diligent

to read Your truth each day,
and help my husband to see its value
and desire it too. Let the wisdom
from the Bible make my marriage
stronger and richer. May I become

a woman of Your Word
in all I say and do.

Marriage is a long-distance race—

and it's uphill most of the way.

Keep investing

110 percent to make your marriage the best it can possibly be.

As positive wives, we can

allow God

to work in and through
our lives
and our marriages in a positive way.

Bring to your marriage
a heart that is inclined
toward God.

Grow spiritually

in your walk with Him,
even if your husband doesn't.
Be a positive influence for your
family, even if your husband
brings negatives.

Being a positive wife
is not about being perfect;
it's about being

faithful

to be who God called us to be
in our marriages.

With a highlighter,

mark the passages
in this book
that have made the greatest impact
on your heart and mind. Write them
on index cards and post them
where you'll see them. May they
encourage you and help give you
strength to be a positive wife.

Heavenly Father, help me to be a
positive influence in my marriage.
Take my gifts and abilities and use
them to be a blessing in my home.

May my words and
actions be a
joyful testimony

of a life lived for Your glory.